A COMMON
NAME *for*
EVERYTHING

∿

A COMMON
NAME *for*
EVERYTHING

Poems

Sarah Wolfson

GREEN WRITERS PRESS | *Brattleboro, Vermont*

Printed in the United States

10 9 8 7 6 5 4 3 2 1

Green Writers Press is a Vermont-based publisher whose mission
is to spread a message of hope and renewal through the words and
images we publish. Throughout we will adhere to our commitment to
preserving and protecting the natural resources of the earth. To that
end, a percentage of our proceeds will be donated to environmental
activist groups. Green Writers Press gratefully acknowledges support
from individual donors, friends, and readers to help support the
environment and our publishing initiative.

Giving Voice to Writers & Artists Who Will Make the World a Better Place

Green Writers Press | Brattleboro, Vermont
www.greenwriterspress.com

ISBN: 978-1-9505841-3-0

COVER ARTWORK:
Crossing the River by Dorothy Caldwell.

For being big sometimes and small at others, in the shadow of the mountains and the shade of the hemlocks.

—BILL MCKIBBEN, *Wandering Home*

CONTENTS

∾

I. HAVE YOU BEEN TO THE PLACE?

II. LITTLE HERE, LITTLE NOW

III. EARTH-THINGS

IV. BEGINNINGS

HAVE YOU
BEEN *to*
THE PLACE?

❧

NIGHT TRAVEL

First lose the light, then the train
and as the great boxed-in shadow of yourselves takes out
whole cornfields, wordlessly agree

to right-crossed journeylegs. Corn.
What's it to you now your shadow snaps in half
the floodlit steeples? Unvisitable towns

wave their plastic welcome mat
at the back of you. Arrival is the new horizon.
Near the door—to what?—the young

stuff their ears and mouths.
When the little trolley rolls up with drinks you think,
tea, what is it? Still here

in seven settings of the sun?
That's when you'll end diversion, use words to decide
who mates with whom and who gets

the last moth-eaten rind. Then it's time to pool
your languages, choose one for housekeeping, one for games,
one to describe the slightest changes in weather.

HAVE YOU BEEN TO THE PLACE?

The one three of anything
from here? You ought to

see it. It's lovely there.
The people may appear

remote, but at heart we're
hearted. If you linger we'll

give you soup and small
theories of holiness. We

have our ways but our small
wooden temples are open

to the wind. Go in, take a cup,
cup a tadpole. Wind greets

nostril no matter how far
from divinity you face. Anoint

yourself with what is close:
pictures of the sleepy saints, steam

off a bovine lip. Have you seen
the place? The children there

are child-sized, the bracken
reluctant to back down.

A STUDY

sought to fuse what we
know about ewes with what

we know about music,
observing a herd of female

ruminants foddered
the tunes of Wagner,

to which they produced
ecstatic milk, whose swells

and lows were enough
to make a lamb choke.

After some turbulent early
hours, however, the lambs

thrived, though little
is known about how allegro

affects the ruminant stomach
in the long term. Of note:

no ewes supernovaed. No soil
rose up and assumed

mammal form. No moons
met earth and two-stepped.

Just sheep, just sheep and
sheep and song. And when

the song ended, just grass
and bats and the loneliness of

dreams, even the realized kind.

AURORA BOREALIS

The summer I was carried half-sleeping to witness,
I thought the house had caught fire. What else
but crisis takes a child

from bed? The pilled nightgown bound

my waist as I was lifted.
Soon I stood balanced on dew, feet
reluctant sponges for the early hours,

surprised to see the lights were green,

not red, not flashing. They danced,
people said, but it wasn't a movement
I could sync with what I knew

of dancing. No siren spun, no ambulance

pulled away in relief or resignation, no hose
extinguished anything. The other onlookers
versed me: it's amazing, their peeled-back lips

let loose, as I strained to see

how all that signaling, shifting light
could have meant marvel, not doom.
Where the horizon should have been

was paneled green. As if at a small thing, I squinted.

Was something closing in? Or ending?
I went from stupor to stupor,
was sent, not carried, back to bed on wet feet,

still shaking from the awful sense of it.

Decades later in plain daylight, I sit
in a red pickup truck in a soup of green
meadows watching a curtain of not quite

white sheep. Now I'm the resounding clown:

*Children! Replace your eyes with tongues
and slurp up sheep!* I seem to say. As if
any multi-stomached truth can be

motion in another's hand. Or mouth.

MY MOTHER NAMES HER INNER STATE

an Atlantic mollusk the way
one might say *my sphagnum*

has lifted. Standing in the dark
shell museum, pointing

at the black and white
Atlantic clam who creates

its variegated shell through
secretion of something

like chalk, she confesses:
Ponderous ark: I feel like one.

An off-center creature
by nature, the ark's a heavy

shell bearing a velvet covering
called *periostracum*. My mother

chooses other words in a world
full enough with language

for all our ills. To calm her young
she offered us the moon. They say

the human ear is more sensitive
year by year. Sometimes I'm

Pluto's moons past my limit. Others
I'm *brimming with jewelweed.*

THE MAMMOTH

After a woman in the village gives birth, a mammoth is placed in the courtyard as a gift and a weight. When strong enough to stand, the mother shuffles over crooked stones through the mossy archway to the mammoth, who waits, head low and inevitable as if surely slaughter will follow, though he knows his mandate: to trap her idle hands. Snails stud his matted coat, which frees the rankness of a hundred eras. His nostrils are the day-god-made-water. If the well went dry, the village could survive a year on his breath. His nose pushes the morning air in small circles, as if to say: *Forget loving all the worldly things: camels and spatulas, the unfolding of a fern, the morning shadow brigade. Now look only to your inner organs.* The mother hangs herself from matted fur by the fingers warming her cheek on the grill of prehistoric ribs. For weeks she is left to do this. People leave food on the ground, but otherwise let her be. Swifts dip in and out in later afternoon. They are the species that doesn't care. Put them on the third day of the universe and they still only narrowly avoid impaling your head, and with perfection. One morning, the mammoth's gone, but even now she creeps out to run her hands through the matted coat, looking to the world like she's combing the air for some small irritant—a wayward milkweed seed, a firefly's defective luminescence.

NO HERON

[The red-winged black bird is a] medium-size passerine with a sharply
pointed, strong bill, somewhat upright posture. Summer male: black,
including soft parts, with bright red shoulder patch or "epaulet,"
bordered by yellow in most subspecies.

—"Red-Winged Blackbird." *National Geographic*

Here, when a baby's eyes
open, they strike red
epaulets on black

and by a nameless
law of metaphysics
all our birds are astral fires

burning up
the firmament.
Elsewhere a hummingbird

darts over a voyager's iceberg
and a vulture, refusing even the stalest cracker,
hisses from some sad lady's gilded cage. But here

all grasses are wheat
and the one passerine (only accidents of dye and heat
could make such scarlet)

dives for frogs, hollows
out a long-dead tree. At night
a tiny haunt, come morning

he mourns dovishly.
So for me,
no heron, no falcon.

No peregrination.
No passage. No pigeon.
No foreign zoo

where popcorn stops the beak
and battens down the wind.
Therefore: no ostrich,

no peacock. Not even the
to-other-eyes ubiquitous
ibis. Not even a pelican

despite the fish
flopping in its throat
like a heart.

OVERWINTERED

Just outside the border
garden, one wayward

crocus emerges first
though each year we hatch

an old fear that this time
it'll be gone like the neighbor's

husband or the old man
across the fence who wrote

in his diary: *tried to fix*
the lawnmower then lay down

forever. There's wonder
in the way his wife tells it,

in her mild avian hand.
Turns out the perambulating

cat is not pregnant, just fat;
that's clear now the snow

doesn't lap her white and low-
hanging belly. Time also

to take stock of friends' bellies,
of the new border gardens of

their eyes: *So much snow in his*
beard! She must know for certain

now she can't have that second
baby. On our side: plaster cracks

and crow's feet. It wasn't long
after the new room was built

that spiders appeared, pale
taupe creatures that live and die

in corners and make
no formal thing of courtship.

FRUITING BODIES

I.
On the third day god created leaf-cutter ants   and said to them
in his stage voice   *go forth and multiply*   and they did. When
they returned   to their maker as if to say   *what next*   god
didn't have a plan for next   so god said offhandedly   *go forth
and find yourselves   what to live in*   and they looked around
and shrugged their thoraxes   and carried off a leaf   carried
it for miles and miles   before stopping briefly to bite it, to spit
it   out and spin it   into a hive of fungal remains of their
total and utter   regurgitation   and established in its orifices
a colony
and settled there
and brought nectar to their queen
whose job it was (because god had not specified)
solely and completely (as the docent put it)
to lay eggs. And this she did
for all the other
18 years she lived.

II.

The father of my offspring tells me   *our bodies are colonies
of individuals* but also *an interesting case of cooperation*   but
he means all our bodies   not just his and mine.   He
speaks also of the *fruiting body*   a blossoming cooperative
of cells that forms   to decide who will propagate and how
the organism will move forward   it's like deciding who gets
sacrificed   *who will fall at the stalk* he says   and *who will form
the fungus flower.*   After unimaginable tragedy   humans are
fond of saying   how will she move forward?   As if one could
get the upper hand   on grief. As if   one could get the upper
hand on grief   by mounting   some human-made vehicle.

III.

My body watches   boggled   the individuals it has inside-
outed.   Not a colony but a cold planet   retreating from
giggling moons. Once a woman   who thought she was dying
was found instead   to have residing in her head   *a clump
of bone, hair, and teeth*   a teratoma, it's called   and apart
from the mental dying   the thing's benign. *Terato*   meaning
monster   but you might also make of it   a terrestrial
sickness   a little earth lump. I like this.   That teeth could
grow erroneously   anywhere in the body is   I believe   part
of upholding a holy order.

IV.
My moons circle farther out   always bouncing back but never
quite as close.   Pluto's in the news again   a projection, a
fruiting body   that never falls off the stalk. Pluto's the victim
in all of us   the mirror   the cheese   in human terms
this means   on earth   we are jumping up and down
screaming to the person next to us   *fly by me   with camera
and telescope   I hold mountains you never knew about.*

LOVE SONG IN A SMALL PLACE

Let there be one place: this clump
of pine we're in. Let the only home

be an old foundation open
to the moon. Pass me the ark

and I'll gobble it. I'm not sorry
for the mess the eager river

has left. Let dragonfly larvae
alight from the lake, let them break

the surface like living shrapnel
released back to seed and forgiven

for the lives ruined. Let this rising
swarm the heavens. Let a pitchfork

be all of these: plow, walking stick,
dancing partner, curmudgeon's brisk

external spine. Come in, perch
on the toadstool while we await

the migration. I'm heating the cauldron;
I'm painting a portrait of god in pine pitch.

My hands are sticky, but, by all means,
move closer. I made this vessel by bending

my own boughs. I'm not sorry for
the starlight, the uneven ground,

or the buzzards in the hinterlands.
On yonder hillside the sheep, I believe,

are happy. If happiness is even a thing
with sheep. If happiness is a thing

with us let this roof open and suck
us out into the starlight. Let there be

one celestial body. Let us knock
the moon off its axis a little. I said

the moon is rising like a dragon.
A great migration is tapping its baton,

cleaning out its sodden hooves. Stir
the pot gently now. The earth's tongues

are reducing into a thicker broth
and no one is losing. It's more savory,

maybe, than you're used to,
but if you have nothing nice to say,

say only one word and let it
be something like waxwing.

LITTLE

HERE,

LITTLE

NOW

❧

A GUIDEBOOK WITH COMMON PHRASES

Colostrum, colloquially beestings (not to be confused with bee stings)
—"Colostrum." *Wikipedia*

The small loft where when it rained the eaves
welcomed the deluge and the owner collected
      this evidence of heavens
         in a sow's trough.   God, colloquially squid.

A small stage where a tall man
soliloquized among fake birches
      with a taxidermy seagull.   Jewelweed, colloquially ink.

The lit kitchen below the hill where
a shared glass of full-fat milk
      was enough adhesive
         for a whole life.   Myrtle, sorrow, splinter.

And despite the call of the mourning dove
         (colloquially dawn, colloquially dusk)
  I love anyone who carries
    a fiddle, who walks
      these hills and pauses on rock
        to speak a creed.

            Child an apple; loss
        a ground-made cider. Return
             another word
        for milk. And who can believe

      my child isn't, at this moment, pumping legs
          through these sodden,
            sainted fields?

APPLES

Men love to tell me
my daughter's name

means little truth
in Latin. Do they love

more the telling or
the naming? Thoreau

(born David Henry)
hewed himself a world

from fake apples:
The Saunterer's Apple

or *malus erronis vel
vagabondi*. Saunterer,

he claimed, emerged
from two words: saint

and terre. It needn't
be true to be so,

he knew. Some days
I could be Catholic,

others I'd lick a bracken
and call it tongue. He called one

Wayside Apple, another
Beauty of the Air.

In fact, her name
means faith in Russian,

something I leave to her
life to unearth. In my mind

(По-моему) this was
Thoreau's best-named fruit:

Our Own Particular
Apple. Little here, little

now, this name says,
a small place's tiny

collaborative anthem,
a homemade person's

tidy bed-borne shape.

ONE PROBLEM WITH MAPS

Here are the woods and a space
big enough to say only that but

not who planted them and what
their fingers look like now and how

many disappointments now pot
the ragweed in their garden plots.

Here are the woods and no room
to proclaim: Observe the woods

of pre-dead deadbeats and small
but joyous heaps of bones, of fish

never for the ocean, of embryonic
wine and the most prodigious spot

of creeping myrtle this side of the
unnamed trickle bountiful in dreams

but barely wet enough for washing up.

GARLIC

Wednesday night chopping garlic
I remember a neighbor, gone now,

who taught me how to slap and flay
the cloves with a knife before mincing.

They say his calf harbored a mass
the size of a grapefruit. I remember how

he wielded steel against earth's smallest,
most pungent segments, smiling out of

his tomato-vined apron. Of sayers,
we say *they*; of ill things, *fruit*. Why

do I want to say *God rest his soul* when
I don't believe in God, only souls, not in

places of rest,   only rest?

WHAT WE TELL CHILDREN ABOUT ANIMALS

The camel keeps water
in his hump, we tell our young

with a certain fervor. Oh yes,
the sloth is lazy and the

elephant never forgets.
Hit a moose with a truck

and the moose will walk
away, we used to say. Then

we got the chance to test
our metal: the car crumpled

and the moose walked
but awfully was how

he did it. Partial leg
to the horizon. After every

nightmare the child rises
calling for her father. The driver

also lived but in still life.
I'm useless with my wan

you'll never leave us. A cricket
brings luck, but the child

makes hers: crouching she plucks
one leaf off every single clover. *Look!*

she calls with real but also
feigned amazement. The bee

dies when it stings, we say;
the bird abandons

a human-scented nest.
More than ever we say,

Watch out for moose. More than ever
I awake with a jolt to August

knowing I have missed
the Perseids. The child

tells me the otter bites
harder than the wolf. That

nothing I can say will
calm her. To which I offer

that ants attend picnics
with something like

religious fervor. That the
cat's tongue is made of tiny

razors. That the ewe will often
nurse another's young.

THE RURAL PANTHEON

An ad's gone out in the village pages
for minor god of incandescent rages.

Likewise sought is someone young and able
to serve as lord of the broken ferry cable,

which is, if all goes well, a temporary job
unlike the spirits of the quaking bog

with positions offered on a rolling basis
to romping boreal waiflike crazies. Praise

the lord of brief but shaming public moments
and glory be to god of smiting garden rodents.

Beware the spirit of dreams involving flight,
for fickle is the goddess of prodigal rights.

NEARER, MY BOG, TO THEE

Psst, Little Bowl of Olympus,
it's me in the bracken bank
flanked by your seraphim sheriffs
light and shade. Looking for you again.
I'd say sun-dappled but precious
little plays upon my face.
A wanderer with torn up legs.
You, my Antique Lady Lake. Oh
Hallowed Carpet! A million emerald
teeth guard your cedar ring but still
it's shrinking. You grow smaller and I
more blundering. There's been lumbering.
I'm bumbling, My Bog, to thee.
I'll decay or eat only cranberries.
The more I ask, the less you exist.
Ribbit. There is only so much holiness.

NAMER OF LAKES

An honest trade.
Like plumbing, passed down
by pedigree and its manifold burdens. Shoes to fill

and shores and shoals and shallows.

And a whole lot of nonsense guidance.
Say water and everyone goes a little bit crazy
in the direction of baptism.

People see me coming and run

for their wheelbarrows. To relocate
a mangy beach. To transplant cattails.
Not anyone can name a lake.

It's not a hunch based on roundness.

Depth must duke it out with weediness,
the drowned man must be forgotten
in favor of general fatality.

I follow my script. Do blueberries exist?

Is the water hospitable
to the pitiable minnow and how long
before fish eggs are swigged

by great predatorial billfulls?

Clay or slate? This is facts,
not character test. The questions
shouldn't keep you up at night.

It's not sea monster and it's not shape.

You don't get to have a vision.
You crunch some numbers,
weigh one strangeness against another.

DECLARED NUISANCES

An unidentified species of bee
flies drunkenly
around the entrance soffits

in early May as if awaiting something

big. She goes
slow
and bumps into things,

including heads, but doesn't

sting. Still,
it's unsettling.
The neighbors' children grow and

grow and nothing

can be done about it.
Mornings
some small material

filters down the walls' interior,

clattering
like grain in a silo,
and it's nothing more than

horse hair that lines the walls

to warm us and muffle
the noise of the neighbors
as they mask their own drunken laughter

with public radio. Sparrows

have imprinted
on the electrical box;
we can't get rid of them

nor their great-grand-kin. It isn't right.

And at night
certain draughts emerge
washing over that act

where, when we inhabitants argue,

we always skew
to the same old crannies
of the kitchen. Out back

the widowed lady, alone in her brick,

hacks limbs
off an old white lilac,
propelled by the gambler's hope

of one last blooming spell.

THE PLACE AND THE WHALE

Once we found a whale in the stubbly
field and assembled to roll it back to

water. In that moment we remembered
we were not a coastal people, couldn't even

pick out the scent of sea. The whale.
Hallucination? Wish? Who needs a reason.

We shared some cheese, touched
our foreheads in disbelief as the children

whirled off to a game, unexplainable
in parts of speech. That was the year

we thought we needed ocean.

FROM ABOVE A LAMBING

With any marvel: the odd
hour. The sun absent, the

barn slant. You're propped
in a half-loft that wouldn't

stop a human child tumbling
onto the hay and birth sac

stage. The sounds: a rustle.
A wet thwump. One bleat

followed by the soft words
of a farmer who'd made this

in every way his living. Something
you did to later say you'd

done it—like drinking slivovitz
or wearing fishnets—watch

a live thing's emerging, face
the odd danger of worlds

opening even as a mostly
lucent bubble still sheathes

some promised creature.

EARTH-

THINGS

SOME CONDITIONS

if you've marveled at the innards of a fig if you've told a fib
if you've bitten into an apple and thought of god if you've
bitten into an apple and thought of the hands that picked
it and placed them on a piano or on your face if you've ever
seen a cardinal and thought fire if you've sewn a seed some
oats and if whenever you encounter a pallet you think palate
tongue lover bed moss if your esophagus is sensitive if you see
in abandoned tractors an extinct species if you have wondered
about the inner lives of museum guards if a pothole takes you
bodily to the moon if your shoes have wings if once you've
loved at an age when all roads lead away from home if you've
tried on another person and were lost if you know that mid-
dles don't fly fletched if you've held a bow and thought of a
book if you've held a book and known the loss of a city if you
have seen fire made from stone and felt thankful to be tempo-
rarily without matches if you know that even the errant leave
footprints if you can't say mud without thinking muddled if
you're a mother if your mouth messes up if idioms are your
houseguests if you ride a lark to work if for the faces of angels
you choose pelicans if you name the large grey moth beat-
ing at your window and listen for patterns in its percussion if
you switch off the light so the moth will find another way if
you believe in ways if you believe in the species if you believe
above all in plural declension if the two words you send to
space are shoal and diphthong if you believe in open-concept
labyrinths in floating the risen rivers if you believe in buzzards
if you believe in cairns and monoliths in stone markers in all
their forms if you believe at any moment any being might
abruptly change direction

LEAVING PANGAEA

Back then we had hearts
the size of watermelons and sweeter.
We waltzed with fruit flies
and root vegetables spoke to us
in their very own organic vowels
of clay and ocean.

A shining wet roof—that is all I remember
from that first trip to the South of France.

In those days we had a tool for taking
the cords off beets. We grew everything,
then, even our little toes. If our noses went
missing we replaced them
with the most obliging grubs we could find.
And they were all obliging. One day

(for there was always something amiss—
a spell of hay fever, the death of a peacock, a lost borzoi)

we were sent out to sea.
Things loomed ahead, large metaphorical
bearded creatures that spoke in low
monosyllabic hums. Murmurs
meant to threaten and reassure.
We traveled on water for days

(I confess I do not believe in time)

upon days. There was no citrus,
no beets. The past flew at us
like an over-eager avian symbol
flapping its too late warning. We got scurvy
and even the weevils were restless.
And then we went on water.

Nothing had changed
except the management and the porch furniture.

And then we went on water.

TO CONSIDER THE TREE CRAB

The mangrove tree crab migrates vertically...
—*"Aratus pisonii." Smithsonian Marine
Station at Fort Pierce*

is to consider the earth
which makes crabs, which makes
trees, which makes oceans
for crabs, and soil for trees.

And after such creation
goes and makes trees grow
from salt water and crabs
to climb them. For a moment

you might not even be
on earth, but no, this is just
a mangrove grove. This is
just a very ordinary planet

whose waters nibble
complicated outcroppings.

VIEWS FROM RUMINANT CREATURES

Oh   impossible world of small gods'   eyes: midnight
mother, alfalfa   and the moon. All algae-bloom   apology
and a traveller   who appears in time for dinner.   Birds in
the rafters   denote ecstatic updrafts. Cubed bread in a basket
stands for a wayward body. Say rain.   Say borne.   Say what
is in the silos.   Say barn fire   over and over   until you
yourself spark.   Then go sleep in the creek bed. What   wafts
from the kitchen wafts from heaven.   Is something only a
visitor says.   The weaver   takes weft to heartstrings   *It's
only yarn It's only yarn*   she sings to sooth herself. The loom
is a harp is a heart. *I love you more   than the space between planets*
claims the child   but   she's uncomfortable knowing   the
center of the planet is liquid.   The cub. The cud. The clubbed
fable, its mossy covers. The collective   bundle. In sunlit cor-
ners   small winter-selves   spin fuzzy, bright omnipotence
on grubby fingers.   In these parts a bump   is considered a
blessing.   Certain birds   says the child   expand the world
with buckthorn.   Say hay.   Say hi.   Say hive.   Say here.

MY FAVORITE HUMAN SMILE

(for the wolf also pulls back lips
against the flesh and the partridge

in her ruffled dotage sits content)
but my favorite human smile hoists

the mouth of one who has just
run for and caught the bus. Specimen:

private glee bent publically,
trumpeting minute derring-do

that in so doing casts bright
relief for the body unmangled

by the moment's folly. A glow
most notable for how fast it fades:

how solemn now the face
as the gray plastic sac settles

in the feet's not-good-enough,
never-good-enough nest.

WE ARE TAKING THE TREES

Grab that large picnic cloth. Gingham unfurled,
moment of person turning bird.

Lay it there. To the right a bit — that's it.
We are taking the ground, its crumb

and piddling creek, its cuddly cave.
Straighten out that corner. Here come the larks

to do as birds in cards and cartoons: alight
in well-trained squadrons

to carry out the calling of their beaks
both funny and hard.

For each lark a corner to be lifted up:
parcel, diaper, kerchief. Not maypole. Not reveler birds

but pretty packing tape. Ballers of root balls,
twitterers from hoe tops and hummocks

soon to hit the fundamental bundle. Large belly
that will doubtless roll away and spill

as soon as we crest the first crab apple hill.
A juncture in good time both funny and hard.

A CHILD TRIES TO EXTINGUISH THE SUN

The child will travel to the sun and back to demand an end to this incessant summer. *Heal, Sun!* she shouts from where she hangs on homemade whirligig wings staring down the lapping flairs, which reach out to harvest or caress her. Over which the sun cannot hear her. Cannot heal her. Later, hungry but undeterred she'll tether herself to the scrubby box elder and hurl twenty-three pails of water skyward. Hurl until her hair is soaked, her shoulder sorer than its small crown of muscle should allow. And barely come in for supper. At dusk she's back to pluck and practicality, making a bow and arrow out of aloe. She works despite the emphatic dark, of which she is not afraid and despite the encircling cicada song, for which she will hereafter bear an abiding terror.

THE SUBTLE ANIMAL

Makes a splash but doesn't
jump. Is that a wing? A tail?

It's hard to tell. She laps milk
from a clamshell with her five-

forked idiom. Her crest and
jowls quiver; her horns twist

too many times around themselves
and often she pauses as if

she's out-paced her subtle
self, but no: this is just one of

many moments not to know.
Somehow the subtle meat

self-pollinates with a sort of
tail not meant for mating.

In times of hate or great
migration, her subtle bones

slacken to newly grounded
shadow. Here she's not scared,

just not so sure her kin have
built the path in relevant relation

to the sun and other bodies,
both celestial and un.

THE MOUNTAIN

We went up the mountain
to see about love. We went
up the mountain to ask
about bears, to play at

Moses. We went to see
remnants, to laugh,
at the summit, at the circled
moon. In the water below,

moon-jellies launch
their throbbing repose.
The valley is covered
in myrtle; the valley

is moldy. From the summit,
tiny laundry flaps its
unheard conversations.
Below, a boulder

tended by gentle junipers
may have been abandoned by
the gods. From here
it's possible to see a time

when even the world's largest
rock ceases. The summit
is covered in lichen. But
what do we know about

how much lichen forms
a covering? We know
about hunger. When we
sit for an apple, fossils

nip our calves. In the past
people went up the mountain
holding tight to flags. From
the summit we construe

the spray of mammals
in the sea. From the summit
the lives of farm hands
look like bliss. We

went up the mountain
to release the dead and
our ghosts which are not
the same. We've lost the trail

on purpose to find
the bog which suggests
another life: not an afterlife,
but the prospect

of a moist, colloidal,
parallel existence. After
the bog the mountain
goes to bramble,

which raises lines
on our still uncertain
legs. What good are we
with our three names

for birds and our zero
language for their songs?
We're up the mountain
to tend something

electric. We carry a hunch
our future may be wrapped
in the whisper of a bear.
We lose the mountain

to find the bramble.
Never mind the blooming
welts on your limbs
and the pulsing

between us. Let it
hang here; let it pause
to drink the pollinated air.
This is the mountain. It may yet

survive the valley. Never mind
the bear beyond me. Forget
the ungodly blackberries
hanging so heavily

they soil themselves
on the earth; forget
the variegated welts
their brambles have embossed

on my wrists. Look here:
at the buttons covering
my ribs, which have,
in our wanderings,

come partway open.

THE PRAYERS OF SHEEP

When a sheep opens its throat
it moves from docile livestock to agonizing,
dying beast. Purr, moan, bellow,
they're all the same: a sheep
when speaking, is always succumbing,
always becoming both more
sheep and more dying.

(And not sheepishly.) Her throat cracks in meadow yodel
as in wolf worry. Death by lightning strike echoes death by
contentment in the clover. Burdock immersion mire musing
alfalfa dilemma heat bleat silage psalm listeria weariness escape
mistake ankle debacle pest protest thistle gristle rain malaise
puddle muddle cottonwood canticle abattoir adieu seclusion
tune strawberry aubade dung song. All easily confused. Sheep
squeezes sheep out into the warm damp barn. Is dying in her
throat as she does it. *Oh my pretty baby* the same song as *oh my
heavy milk*. And when a sheep prays it is always *god help me: I
must split myself open to ask of you anything.*

I used to loath
academics' hegemonic kingdoms,
the gussied up language
for *blueberries
grow from good earth.*
Eat it, I thought, or at least
call it what it is. Then
I found the word
Weltschmerz. Now I know
we must all find our own ways
to take ourselves
too seriously.

BEGINNINGS

❧

THE PROPAGULE

Like most mammals, mangroves are viviparous (bringing forth live young), rather than producing dormant resting seeds like most flowering plants. Mangroves disperse propagules via water with varying degrees of vivipary or embryonic development while the propagule is attached to the parent tree.
—"Reproductive Strategies of Mangroves."
Newfound Harbor Marine Institute

The mangrove spawn,
a sideways (sort-of)
seed, floats and bobs
in the world where
everything's an egg,
(almost) as for the child
who peered over a nest's
edge and—present!—
three blue eggs so real
as to be candy. He didn't
eat. The mangrove pod
bobs and weaves until
it settles rather than
dives sideways on a
habitable spit of sand,
the propagule a kind of
roving ovary, a buoyant
earth-berry in a way,
(if everything's an egg,
everything has one),
an ore that varies
by territory and weather,
an ur-rover, a veritable
apiary (almost), an ova,
a reed, a doe, a ray, and
a—forgive me—a me.

REGENERATION (ACORNAL, CORALIC, HUMAN)

With human spawn, apples
fall in certain proximity

to the tree (let that be
a toast: to thee, the tree!)

or are sheep of another
type, while acorns, born,

fall and are born(e again)
by circumstances beyond

gravity, e.g. mandibularity
of small mammals or fatted

toddler claw. And coral
by another grace remakes

itself: not birth nor fall nor
fume nor maw. Sumich (1996)

suggests new coral bits
bud off from parent polyps

to expand or begin new colonies
when the *parent...reaches*

a certain size and divides.
So: newness without

novelty or breakage.
But oh, how humans

love that old roots and
wings cliché. It's hard

to get rid of. Like a
stray. Like a child

you have raised in the
wrongish sorts of ways.

AN UNFUNDED STUDY OF MILKING
AND THE MOON

Nursing wounds are preferable to bites
by Beringian lions and scimitar cats

whose large eyes and pivot speed
would have allowed them to hunt skillfully

on moonless nights such as in Pleistocene
Yukon. In fact, mammoths may have

nursed themselves to death according to
new research by Jessica Metcalfe

of the University of Western Ontario,
which suggests that all those long dark

ice age nights were spent clustering
in intense lactation, that to feed

their young, the species needed
to wait out the dark in a way. Metcalfe

calls this *behavioural adaptation to…*
winter darkness and hypothesizes

that such long periods of stillness
made mammoths more vulnerable

to hunting by, among other things,
humans. I am done milking and my children,

my kind, have so far survived, but
there's a wound here somewhere

I'm trying to salve or save for *consumption*
later in life which, in Metcalfe's view,

is what the mammoths did with leaves:
In the long winter darkness,

vegetation was sparse and so
the young megaherbivores,

as they are known, ate no greens
until age two or sometimes three.

Metcalfe acknowledges poetry a little
when she concedes all estimates about

mammoth tooth growth must first
go through what we know about

the African Elephant. Metcalfe is herself
an ungulate in name. I imagine

it must be hard to love without the moon.
For Metcalfe, I assume, dating is mostly

the radiocarbon variety, but who's to say
what is and isn't propagatory. Love is

an easy, dark pursuit, a thin
grasp at a hint and let that be

nourishment. I am from where
generations make a living

on milk. We have the moon, we have
our seasons. Our predators

are few but to make this milking
happen someone has to want it

to go on. If you can't have sleep,
have extinction. Ask any new mother

about long winter nights. If by chance
the child sleeps, your lions lie with you,

awake and needy, and even if through skill
you calm them, there's always that one

piece of moonlight come to pose
its stubborn Pleistocene questions.

BIRTH STORY

As the sun broke loose over metal girders, a hundred men
in hard hats were already pounding outside the window,
slowly coming down with cancer. A nurse went rotely

about her drudgery, her mind on her mother's memory.
And my son emerged in the middle of a lesson
on flexibility under duress as the obstetrician

schooled the resident on the sutures of the human skull.
Language like *sphenoethmoidal* floated closer than my
heartbeat to his auroral ears, its own virtuosic music,

a tune people make for parts of people. I was there, too,
attending to waves and circumstances, demanding
wool socks like the world depended on them. I could say

honestly: take your time, obstetrician and tenderfoot
resident, go slow soft-headed baby. I can wait
while you teach and learn and linger. The midwife

had warned that hospital birth means being among
strangers at life's most unmasked moment, but
I suppose that means she believes in strangers.

AN UNFUNDED STUDY OF THE AFTERBIRTH

When it had been seen to
    that the grayness had
        receded, that the birthed

could breathe and suck, that
    the mother had uptaken
        several stitches of a fiber

as powerful in every sense as
    spider silk, that the after-pain
        had shrunk down to a boot

abandoned in a puddle,
    the child who would sooner
        than I could know spin phrases

like "I'll heal" and "I hate
    you" slept with contentment
        uncharacteristic of her recent

world-leap. Then, when the bustle
    relaxed into coffee and crosswords,
        and the nurse turned on her lazy

ether of success tossed with
    almost finished, almost perfect paperwork,
        I asked to see the placenta.

They brought it smooth side up,
    bearing it like friendly handmaids
        but also perfunctorily as if to say:

this is a duty and a game;
smell the wine but don't
complain. It was red, of course,

the red of held-togetherness,
the red of monk-trampled
cordial, and smooth as all

get-out. It might have been
the moon, not the hidden, snarled
rootball of its underside. I liked it.

It looked fine in its stainless
steel pan. It glowed, but I didn't
want to take it home.

ARRIVAL AT THE RIVER JORDAN

dark ridges broke the water
no one had mentioned

the alligators

though there they were
swimming in obelisks
performing the columns and paisley twists

of ancient pottery — this

just at the moment
we should carnally forget
those devoted friends

our heel thorns and the side stitches
not yet attributable
to laughter and

with joy unheralded

jump in

now how we laughed
let it rip loose
our collective umbilicus
pop open our ribs

alligators?
at the font of afterlife?

who was angry with us?

the local adolescents?
universal holiness?

or was it a vision
suggesting
something of an alligator

in us?

THE LANDING

The shore rose up and found us, an island narrowly,
in truth a private compost heap pricking
the surface of the sea. The sound: melamine

etching a tree the bees have wholly turned
to honey, the lurch worse than a flock of
vengeful cuckolds though our vessel

dwarfed the land one hundredfold. To disembark
on this microscopic spit? What roots
accept such shallowness and still bear fruit?

We got out. Knee deep in resurrection muck.
Sifted. Raked. Stayed. Built hills of guilt
and forgiveness wherever there was space.

RENOVATION

Today I unloaded the
cupboard; yesterday

you left a wet cloth
in that mountain-cave

arrangement on the tub.
The space we roost in

shakes differently than
before though last night

we had the same old talk
about how to occupy it

better together. In the
morning a man climbs

through the window with
a tool made both for building

and tearing down. He's happy
in his work, a happiness he'll pass

to his children, but I imagine
he hits his wife. Back when

the young slept, we argued
in the closet where shoes

are not too tidily kept.
Nowadays they are awake

and roar back. Next week
the house will again make contact

with the ground; the cracks
will be filled, the squirrels corralled

to hold their circus
elsewhere. Another man

will come and will cement
something. They'll remove

the safety net and close us
back in. Then the sounds of

us will echo off our own
walls only, the localest species

dipping fast and low and only
narrowly missing our heads,

as we humans like to say.

A SMALL AND UNSUCCESSFUL RECKONING

A neighbor attempts
to evict house finches

nesting in his awning
by suspending silver strips

like pennants at a jeep
dealership. He blows air

into inflatable owls,
dismantles inaugural nests

of twig and stem and string
with Bar-B-Q tongs. Does

daily penance in the chapel
of his head for standing

in the way of egg-laying.
Nothing gives. Resigned

to his plastic Adirondack
chair, he sips beer and flips

the tongs like a juggling pin.
In another place, The Great

Pacific Garbage Patch sways
the way Thich Naht Hanh

says one should meditate.

THE AFTERLION

always a lion
(though always the zoo is gutted)
wanders through this scene:

the empty seething streets

and though he might
he doesn't stumble over wayward steel
or melting stone

but clearly something in his paw's not right

his black-gold mane is now
the black-gold flame
that licked and let him loose

the donkeys? eaten
parrots? phoenixed dashingly away
no currency for elephants perhaps

or the prized one died on impact

but the lion takes on time
doesn't die
is what everyone remembers and none have seen:

his tail that morning swishing
through the iron gate
later in the street him feasting

on what rot is to be found in hindsight

even yesterday
his orchid tongue
lapping plainly from the river

THE NEXT SEASON

In our dreams the moose
gets up and backs away and away and away, his leg

as it should be, his hulk
unbumped. The smell of cedar is also the shape of

cedar: and here now is a new
world order and the child can say a little longer what it is

she needs to wonder and still
there's some summer left in which to connect a comet

to any single mammal sense.
And the lion will lie down with the lamb. And the bird

will roost in a human-
scented nest. And the loon lowers herself for her babies.

And now: August
with its great star events, each night of which I have awoken

hungry and remembered
to walk out unblinking into the warm and vigorous night.

NOTES & ACKNOWLEDGEMENTS

∾

I gratefully acknowledge the editors of the following journals in which some of these poems first appeared, sometimes in slightly different forms:

AGNI, "Night Travel"

Bennington Review, "Some Conditions"

Contemporary Verse 2, "The Rural Pantheon"

Gulf Coast, "We Are Taking the Trees"

jubilat, "Views from Ruminant Creatures"

Michigan Quarterly Review, "An Unfunded Study of the Afterbirth"

Mid-American Review, "Namer of Lakes"

National Poetry Review, "My Favorite Human Smile"

PRISM International, "Regeneration (Acornal, Coralic, Human)"

Radar Poetry, "A Study," "From Above a Lambing," "The Subtle Animal," "The Propagule," and "The Landing"

Room, "Declared Nuisances"

Saranac Review, "The Mountain"

Scrivener Creative Review, "Love Song in a Small Place"

Spinning Jenny, "Leaving Pangaea"

The Fiddlehead, "Apples" and "Overwintered"

The Puritan, "The Next Season" (appeared as "Revision")

Tupelo Quarterly, "No Heron" and "The Afterlion"

West Branch, "Fruiting Bodies"

I would like to thank the Quebec Writers' Federation for its generous support. Many peers, teachers, and mentors have nurtured my work and poetic outlook: my thanks to all of them. In particular, I'm grateful to Rachel Nelson, Katie Umans, Rae Gouirand, Ryan Flaherty, andrea bennet, Phil Crymble, and Darcie Dennigan: your feedback and encouragement have been invaluable. My deep gratitude goes to Artley, Rich, and Carrie Wolfson for their love and support. Finally, to Gary, language enthusiast and appreciator of the arts, thank you for your steadfast patience and love. This book is dedicated to you and to our homemade persons: Vera, whose name means *faith* in Russian, and Leo Henry, named in part for the man who sauntered.

In "Overwintered," the last line is adapted from Anita Carpenter's "Daddy Long Legs" (*Wisconsin Natural Resources Magazine.* Wisconsin Department of Natural Resources, June 2000. Web.).

"Fruiting Bodies" uses language from the article "Woman's Brain Tumor Turns out to Be 'evil Twin' Complete with Bone, Hair and Teeth" (*Washington Post.* 23 April 2015. Web.) and from a personal interview with Gary Brouhard (23 July 2015).

In "Apples," Thoreau's names for apples were found in Robert

D. Richardson's *Henry Thoreau: A Life of the Mind*. (University of California Press, 1986).

In "Leaving Pangaea" the italicized lines are from Vladimir Nabokov's *Speak Memory: An Autobiography Revisited*. (Vintage, 1989).

Language in "Views from Ruminant Creatures" was inspired by Don Mitchell's *Flying Blind: One Man's Adventures Battling Buckthorn, Making Peace with Authority, and Creating a Home for Endangered Bats*. (Chelsea Green Publishing, 2013).

"An Unfunded Study of Milking and the Moon" was inspired by and uses language from Jessica Z. Metcalfe et al.'s article "Nursing, Weaning, and Tooth Development in Woolly Mammoths from Old Crow, Yukon, Canada: Implications for Pleistocene Extinctions." (*Palaeogeography, Palaeoclimatology, Palaeoecology*. 2010. Web.).

In "Regeneration (Acornal, Coralic, Human)" the italicized lines are from the article "How Do Corals Reproduce?" (*NOAA Ocean Service Education*. National Oceanic and Atmospheric Administration, 21 July, 2009. Web.).

SARAH WOLFSON's poems have appeared in Canadian and American journals including *AGNI, The Fiddlehead, Michigan Quarterly Review, PRISM international,* and *TriQuarterly*—and they have twice been nominated for a Pushcart Prize. She holds an MFA from the University of Michigan. Originally from Vermont, she now lives in Montreal, where she teaches at McGill University.

A Common Name for Everything was typeset in Dante, a serif book typeface designed by Giovanni Mardersteig for the Officina Bodoni in the mid-20th century. Its roots, however, can be traced to the 15th-century type cuts of Francesco Griffo. One of Mardersteig's main design goals for Dante was to visually harmonize the roman and italic styles, which cuts from Griffo's era did not. Although initially designed for the individual handpress, Dante was soon issued for machine composition and later redrawn for digital use.

෴

Design by Dede Cummings
Brattleboro, Vermont